WHAT DOES A FORWARD DO?

Paul Challen

PowerKiDS press.
New York

I0811123

Published in 2018 by The Rosen Publishing Group, Inc.
29 East 21st Street, New York, NY 10010

Copyright © 2018 by The Rosen Publishing Group, Inc.

All rights reserved. No part of this book may be reproduced in any form without permission in writing from the publisher, except by a reviewer.

Developed and Produced for Rosen by BlueApple*Works* Inc.
Managing Editor for BlueApple*Works*: Melissa McClellan
Art Director: Tibor Choleva
Designer: Joshua Avramson
Photo Research: Jane Reid
Editor: Marcia Abramson

Photo Credits: Cover left Peter Muzslay/Dreamstime.com; cover right Hasan Shaheed/Shutterstock; title page muzsy/Shutterstock; TOC, p. 26 Noah Salzman/Creative Commons; TOC background, background p. 8, 10, 14, 16, 20, 22, 26, 30, 32 romakoma/Shutterstock; page numbers EFKS/Shutterstock; top backgrounds p. 4, 8, 10, 14, 16, 20, 22, 26 Christian Bertrand/Shutterstock; backgrounds 6, 7, 12, 13, 18, 19, 24, 25, 28, 29 odd-add/Shutterstock; p. 4, 5, 7 TJ Choleva; p. 6, 19 Mitch Gunn/Shutterstock; p. 8 Naci Yavuz/Dreamstime.com; p. 9 ristiano barni/Shutterstock; p 9 top lev radin/Shutterstock; p. 10 Stef22/Dreamstime.com; p. 11 Celso Pupo Rodrigues/Dreamstime.com; p. 12 MediaPictures.pl/Shutterstock; p. 13 Keeton10/Dreamstime.com; p. 14 A_Lesik/Shutterstock; p. 15 Jaggat Rashidi/Shutterstock; p. 15 top left Jenta Wong/Dreamstime.com; p. 15 top right Cosmin Iftode/Dreamstime.com; p. 16 Mitchell Gunn/Dreamstime.com; p. 17 AGIF/Shutterstock; p. 17 top Stef22/Dreamstime.com; p. 18 Keeton10/Dreamstime.com; p. 20, 24, 27 right, 30 MaxiSports/Dreamstime.com; p. 21 Aspenphoto/Dreamstime.com; p. 21 top Neil Harrison/Dreamstime.com; p. 22, 23 Dziurek/Shutterstock; p. 22–23 top Christian Bertrand/Shutterstock; p. 25 Vasilis Ververidis/Dreamstime.com; p. 26 right Fernando Frazão/Agência Brasil/Creative Commons Attribution 3.0 Brazil; p. 27 left mooinblack/Shutterstock; p. 27 top Jerry Coli/Dreamstime.com; p. 28 Michael Chamberlin/Shutterstock; p. 29 Wallenrock/Shutterstock; back cover Krivosheev Vitaly

Cataloging-in-Publication Data
Names: Challen, Paul.
Title: What does a forward do? / Paul Challen.
Description: New York : PowerKids Press, 2018. | Series: Soccer smarts | Includes index.
Identifiers: ISBN 9781508154495 (pbk.) | ISBN 9781508154457 (library bound) | ISBN 9781508154372 (6 pack)
Subjects: LCSH: Soccer--Juvenile literature.
Classification: LCC GV943.25 C53 2018 | DDC 796.334'64--dc23

Manufactured in China

CPSIA Compliance Information: Batch #BS17PK For Further Information contact: Rosen Publishing, New York, New York at 1-800-237-9932

CONTENTS

THE SOCCER TEAM 4

THE FORWARD LINE UNIT 6

FORWARD SETUPS 8

FORWARD SKILLS 10

STRIKERS 12

WINGERS 14

TARGET PLAYERS 16

AERIAL THREAT 18

FALSE NINES 20

GOAL POACHERS 22

THE ROLE OF A HEAD COACH 24

THE BEST FORWARDS 26

BE A GOOD SPORT 28

GLOSSARY 30

FOR MORE INFORMATION 31

INDEX 32

THE SOCCER TEAM

Eleven players make up a soccer team. Two teams play a game of soccer. Each team has a goalkeeper, the one player who remains in the goal and tries to keep the other team from scoring. The rest of the soccer team's players can move all over the field. Defenders, midfielders, and forwards — the 10 remaining outfield players — can play in many different formations.

A soccer team's formation is described using numbers. Starting with the number of defenders , then midfielders, and then the forwards, this system describes how a team will set up. A common 4-5-1 formation means that, along with the goalkeeper, a team will play with four defenders, five midfielders, and one attacking forward.

4-5-1 Formation

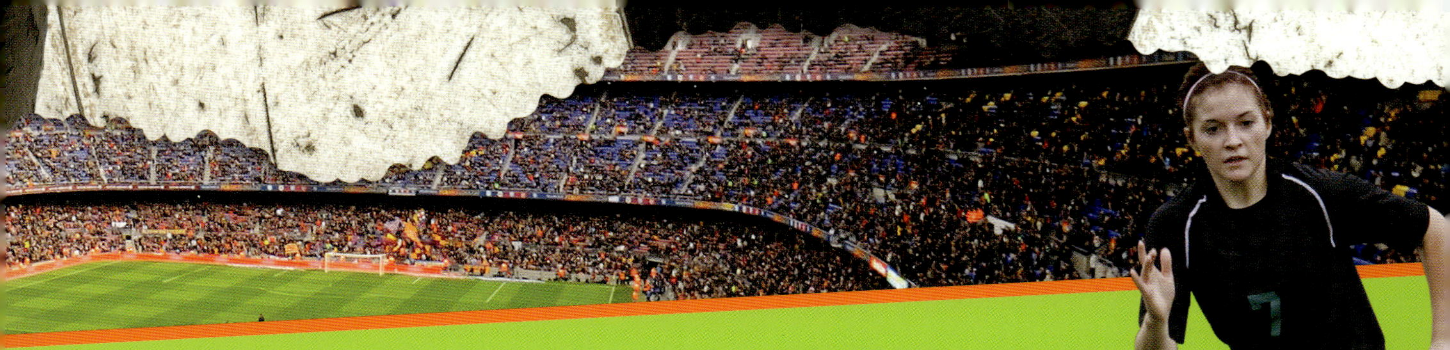

THE ROLE OF THE FORWARD

The forwards are the main attacking players on a team. Their number one job is to score and set up goals to help their team win. Although forwards do have other important jobs on a soccer team, they're on a team to score! Because forwards do play such an important role in attacking, they are often the most popular players among soccer fans.

The soccer field is often called the pitch by fans and players. It has two goals on either side. End lines run behind each goal, and sidelines run along the sides. Corner flags and markings are in each of the four corners. Each goal has a 6-yard box, a penalty spot, and an 18-yard box in front of it. The center circle is right in the middle of the field.

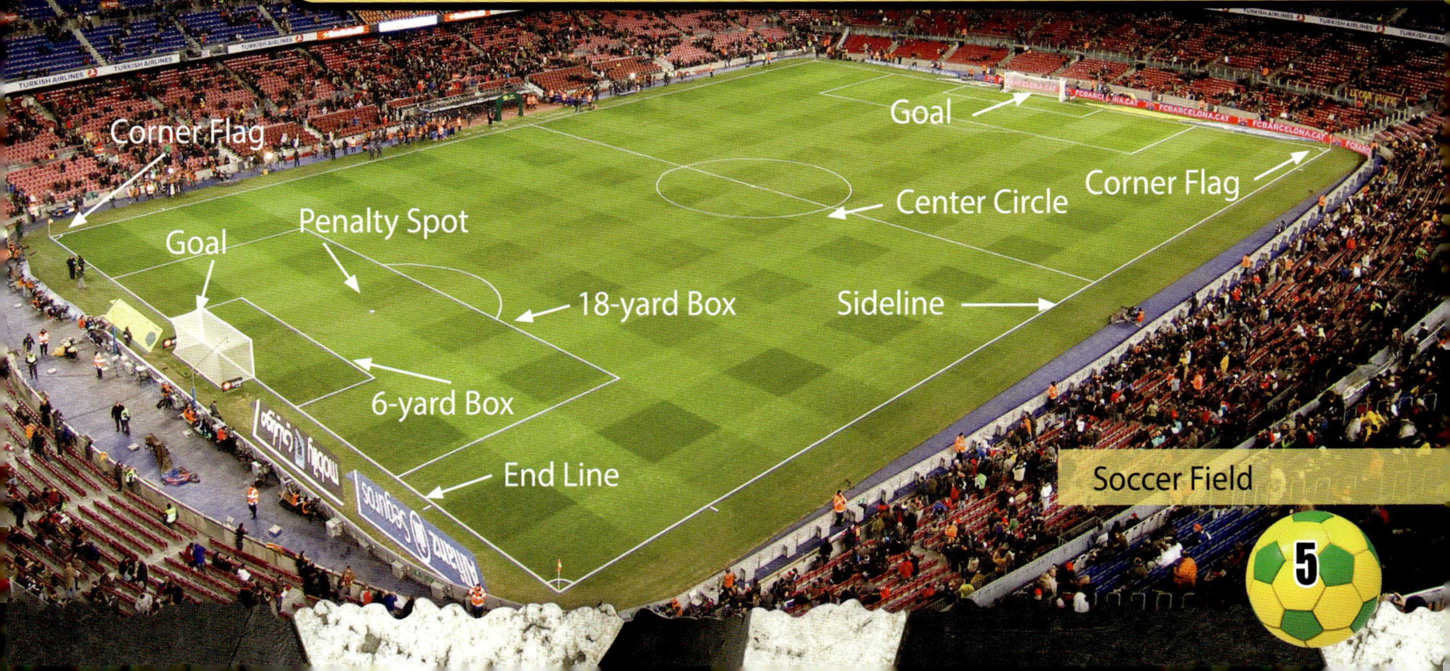

Soccer Field

THE FORWARD LINE UNIT

Of the three lines of players on a soccer pitch, the forward line plays closest to the opposing goal. Defenders stay closest to a team's own goal, with the midfielders in between. Of course, these positions are always shifting as players run up and down the field. In general, though, forwards will always be the players nearest the opponent's goal.

Forwards mainly look to score and set up goals, so coaches usually play their most offensive-minded players in these positions.

*Players who love to shoot and **dribble** past opponents make ideal forwards.*

Coaches can put as many forwards as they like on the field at any one time. Typical formations have one, two, or three forwards based on the overall game strategy. If a team's strength is in defense, it may want to use only one player as a forward, choosing to concentrate more on stopping the opponent than on scoring goals. If a team wants to score lots of goals, three forwards may make more sense.

In the modern game of soccer, coaches want forwards to contribute to the team by "tracking back," or running to a defensive position when the opponent has the ball.

Teams that play with three forwards, such as a 4-3-3 formation, usually set up with one center forward and two wingers.

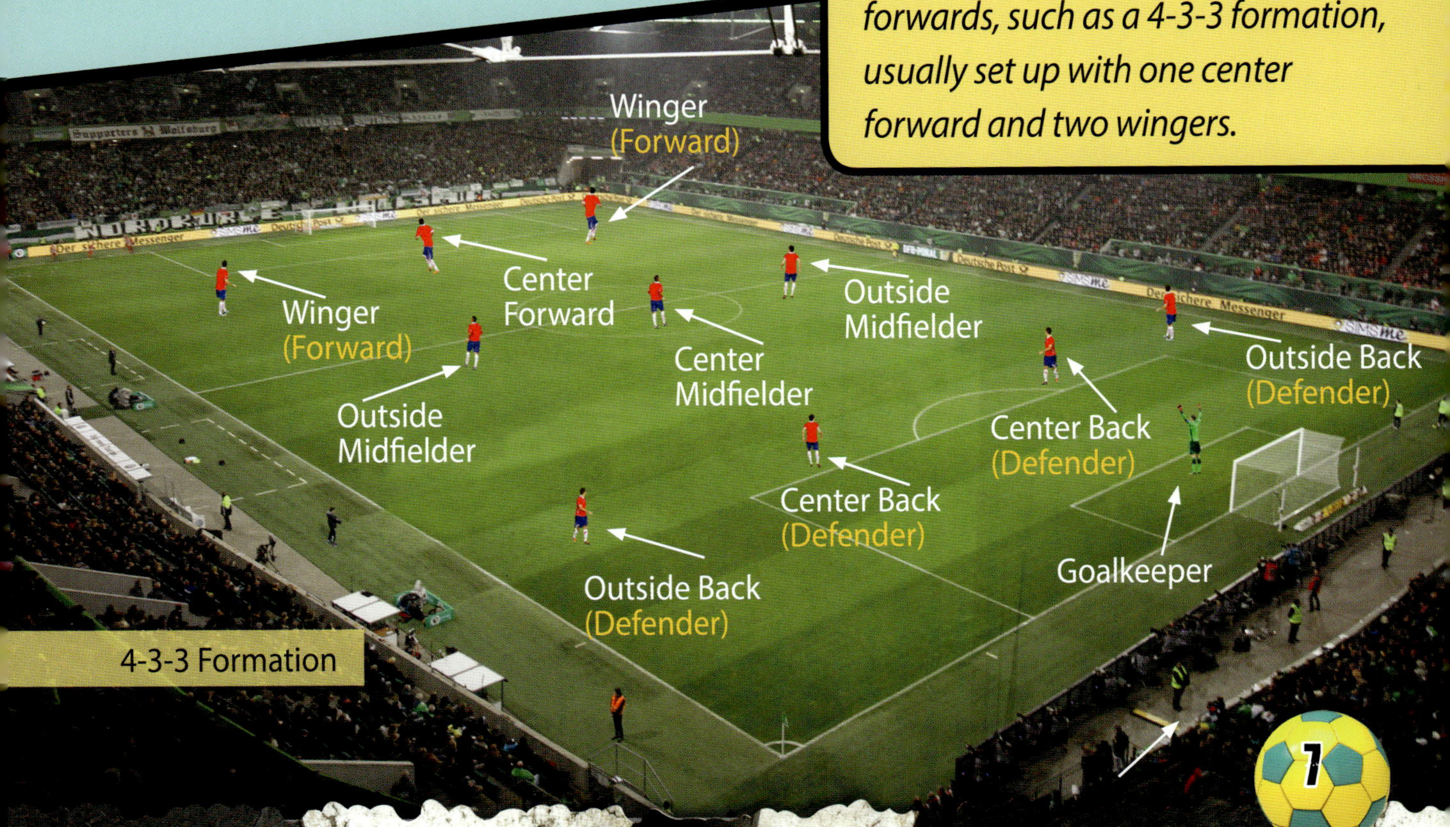

FORWARD SETUPS

There are two main kinds of forwards. Those who play mostly in the middle part of the pitch are called center forwards, or strikers. Forwards who play on the outsides of the pitch, or "on the wings," are known as wingers.

Typically, strikers are strong, tall players who play near the opposing goal and use their size and strength to score. However, there have been many great strikers who have been smaller, quicker players.

Usually, wingers are players who love to dribble and try to beat opposing defenders with speed and trickery.

DID YOU KNOW?

You don't have to be big to be a great striker! One of the most exciting players in Major League Soccer, Sebastian Giovinco (also known as the Atomic Ant), is only 5-foot-4 (1.6 m) but led the league in scoring in his first season. Playing for Toronto, he won the Most Valuable Player award as well.

TWO UP FRONT

A common midfield formation is to play with two strikers who work in combination with one another. One of these strikers is often a tall, powerful player with a good shot and strong heading skills. The other is often smaller and quicker. Pairing "little and large" players this way can give a team a balanced attack.

If a team does use this kind of "strike partnership," it will usually sacrifice one player from the midfield to have this extra center forward. For this reason, it is very important that the two strikers communicate and work together well.

Many of soccer's greatest two-striker matchups have been players with an amazing ability to "read" one another's movements and habits on the pitch.

FORWARD SKILLS

Because they are always looking to score, forwards need top-notch offensive skills. These include the ability to dribble in tight spaces past defenders and a range of powerful and accurate shots. All forwards, and especially wingers, need great speed and trickery to beat defenders in the open field, and must make quick decisions under pressure. Forwards must also know how to work well with teammates through accurate passing and smart runs when they don't have the ball.

Forwards must have the ability to receive passes on the ground and in the air, and the control to fire off quick shots.

EYE FOR GOAL

Soccer fans like to say that the best forwards have an "eye for goal." This means they can anticipate passes and shoot accurately. A key part of this is "reading" goalkeepers to see where they are positioned and to shoot away from them. This usually has to be done very quickly, so an eye for goal must also be combined with quick movements.

A lot of the work a forward must do to score happens without the ball. Experienced strikers make all sorts of runs to get themselves open to receive passes from teammates. This is hard work, especially since a striker can spend many minutes running without the ball just to get one goal-scoring chance.

One of the key skills top forwards have is the ability to split defenders with runs and dribbling. This can mean finding the space between two opponents and running through it to receive a pass.

STRIKERS

Sometimes called center forwards, strikers play in the middle of the offensive part of the field. Central strikers are the players on a team who are mainly responsible for scoring. They use all kinds of skills, such as heading, shooting, and **volleying**, in all kinds of different offensive situations to try to score. On corner kicks and free kicks, strikers will often be targets for high balls. They try to use these opportunities to score.

Some fans also call the striker the number nine player because in one system of numbering the 11 players on the field, the striker is always number nine.

STRIKER SKILLS

The most important skills a striker can have are known as finishing skills — the ones a player needs to convert a goal-scoring chance into a goal. Good strikers can control passes with many different body parts, and can shoot accurately and powerfully with both feet and their heads.

Strikers must know how to shield the ball from defenders with their bodies, and how to find space to receive passes in scoring areas. They must also know how to hit long and short passes accurately.

Strikers need good dribbling skills to baffle defenders with the ball at their feet.

WINGERS

Wingers are forwards who play wide on the field and often start their attacks along the sidelines. Wingers use speed and dribbling to beat defenders. When they get close to goal, they can cut to the center part of the field to try to score, or pass to teammates to set them up for scoring chances. Wingers also need to do a lot of running off the ball to free themselves up to receive passes from teammates, and to defend against opposing wide players.

Many coaches teach wingers to get "chalk on the boots." This means that the winger sets up so wide on the field that they are pressed right to the sideline, which in earlier times was marked with white chalk.

DID YOU KNOW?

Soccer fans around the world love to debate which striker is the world's best player. For men's soccer, some say it is the lightning quick goal-scoring machine Cristiano Ronaldo (7) of Portugal. Others say it is the tricky dribbling artist Lionel Messi (10) of Argentina. The two are always at or near the top of the annual goal-scoring charts in the Spanish league, where Ronaldo plays for Real Madrid and Messi for Barcelona.

Above all, wingers need to have great dribbling skills and ball control. They must be able to execute these skills at great speed to beat defenders. Wingers also need to be able to deliver accurate **crosses** through the air to teammates waiting near the goal. To do all this, wingers need to have great endurance.

Wingers need to master a range of short and long passes to connect with teammates and to make runs with the ball.

TARGET PLAYERS

Some coaches set up their teams by placing a single striker far up the pitch to act as a target for long passes. Rather than taking the pass and bursting forward to attack, this target player aims to control the ball and pass to one of several teammates who are running forward to join the offensive efforts. This is a tough job because the target player is often alone as the highest player up the pitch, and must hold off defenders looking to win the ball.

Target, or hold-up, players are often tall and physically strong. They have good ball control and passing skill. They also must be very patient, because their chances to score often come after a lot of hard work trying to win the ball and combining with teammates through passing.

DID YOU KNOW?

Strikers around the world love to do funny dances and celebrations after scoring. Backflips, belly flops, and using the corner flag as an air guitar are all popular ways to show the crowd they are happy they have scored. When playing a game away from home, some strikers run down the pitch with a finger to their lips as they "shush" the crowd. One of the best goal celebrations is the one that skinny Peter Crouch of England does — a jerky "robot dance" that always has the crowd laughing.

To be a good target player, you need to be good at controlling balls in the air with the head, chest, and other body parts. Target players need to know how to shield the ball away from defenders with their bodies, and must be skilled passers. These players also must have a lot of patience, endurance, and discipline to be successful at this position.

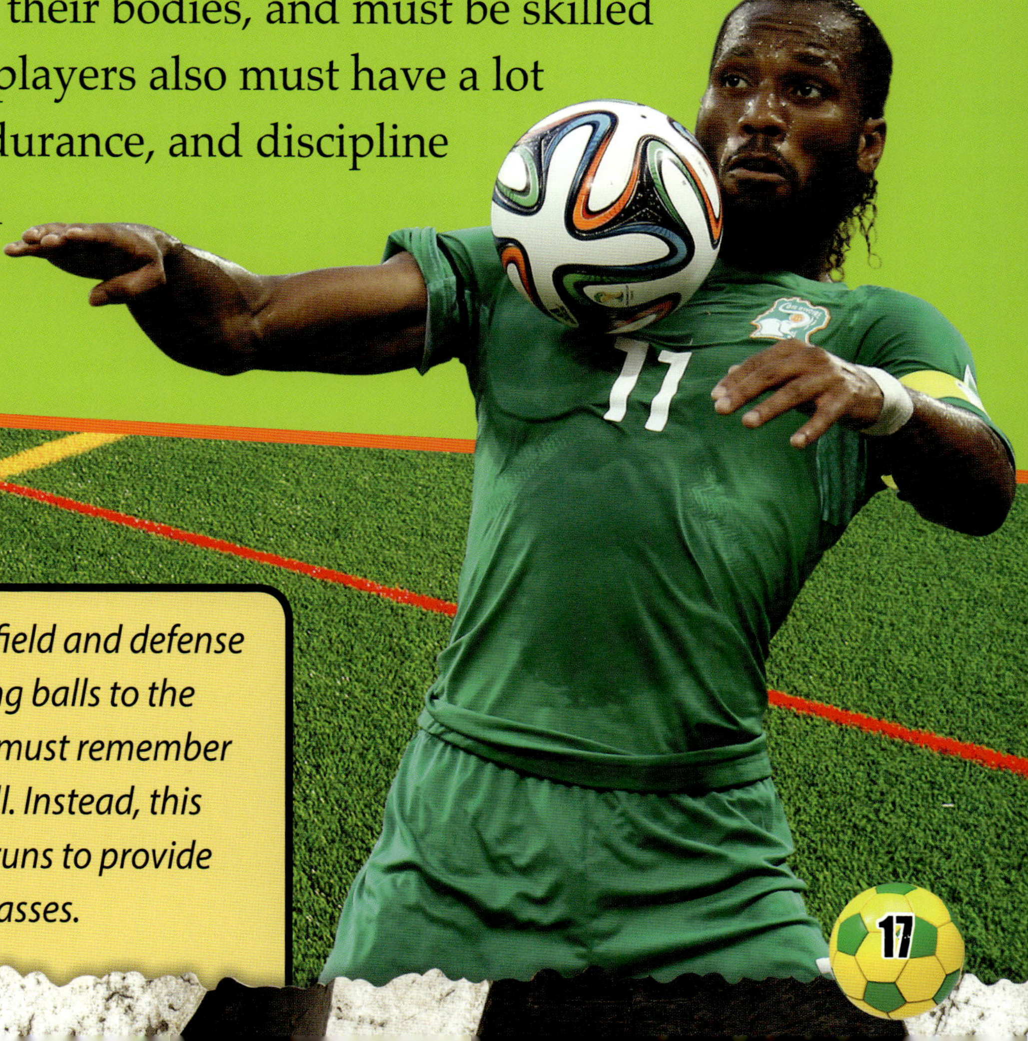

Teammates in midfield and defense will look to play long balls to the target player, who must remember never to remain still. Instead, this player must make runs to provide a good target for passes.

AERIAL THREAT

Forwards, especially strikers, are often in the center of the action on corner kicks and free kicks — and when crosses come into the goal area. Teammates count on these players to use their jumping skills, strength, and often their height to head the ball towards the goal to try to score. Often, strikers who are strong in the air are able to use their agility to win these aerial balls over challenging defenders who are trying to clear the ball away from goal.

Strong jumping skills are key to good headers. Timing the jump just right is important so the striker is not heading the ball on the way down, which can lessen the hit's power.

Players with strong header skills make contact on the ball with their foreheads for maximum impact. They can also generate power into their headers by using their neck muscles to snap their heads forward onto the ball as it arrives.

Some strikers also try to "flick on" aerial balls with their heads. The aim here is not necessarily to score, but to change the direction of the ball with the side of the head so it lands at the feet or head of a teammate who is waiting near the goal and ready to score. Being able to flick on an aerial ball is difficult but is a great way for a forward to get an **assist** on a goal.

Sometimes, a cross comes in so fast that, rather than trying to put power into a header, a striker will simply let it glance off the side of the head, redirecting it to the goal.

FALSE NINES

Soccer fans have been referring to strikers as number nines for a long time, but in recent years, a new kind of player has emerged — the **false nine**. These players are still expected to be goal scorers, but it's also common for them to drop deeper into midfield to receive passes and start attacks. In fact, the false nine position is really a combination of a striker and an attacking midfielder.

World-class false nines, such as Lionel Messi (left) of Barcelona and Argentina, and Karim Benzema (right) of France and Real Madrid, help their teams by passing, creating, and scoring goals.

DID YOU KNOW?

Ivory Coast striker Didier Drogba is such a hero in that country that his appeal for peace in a post-game speech actually stopped a civil war there. In 2006, during the qualifying tournament for the World Cup, Drogba made an appearance on television, asking the government of the Ivory Coast to stop the fighting and try to resolve the country's problems by calling an election.

False nines combine the offensive qualities of a midfielder and a striker, so these players must have skills that are suited for both positions. They must have the midfielder's ability to pass with both feet over short and long distances, and the vision to read the game. They must also be able to dribble at a fast speed to create chances to score for teammates. Like a good striker, the false nine must have good heading skill to convert crosses and free kicks into goals.

False nines also must be able to shoot accurately and hard, both after beating opponents with turns and dribbles, and after receiving passes from teammates.

GOAL POACHERS

Some strikers seem to do only one thing for their team — score goals. These players are not especially helpful on defense, and can seem to "disappear" for long stretches of time in matches, only to suddenly appear by scoring a goal — or several. Although it is not a formal term for a type of soccer forward, most soccer fans know these players are called **goal poachers**.

*Forwards are often called to contribute their skills to **set pieces** such as corner kicks, free kicks, and **penalty kicks**.*

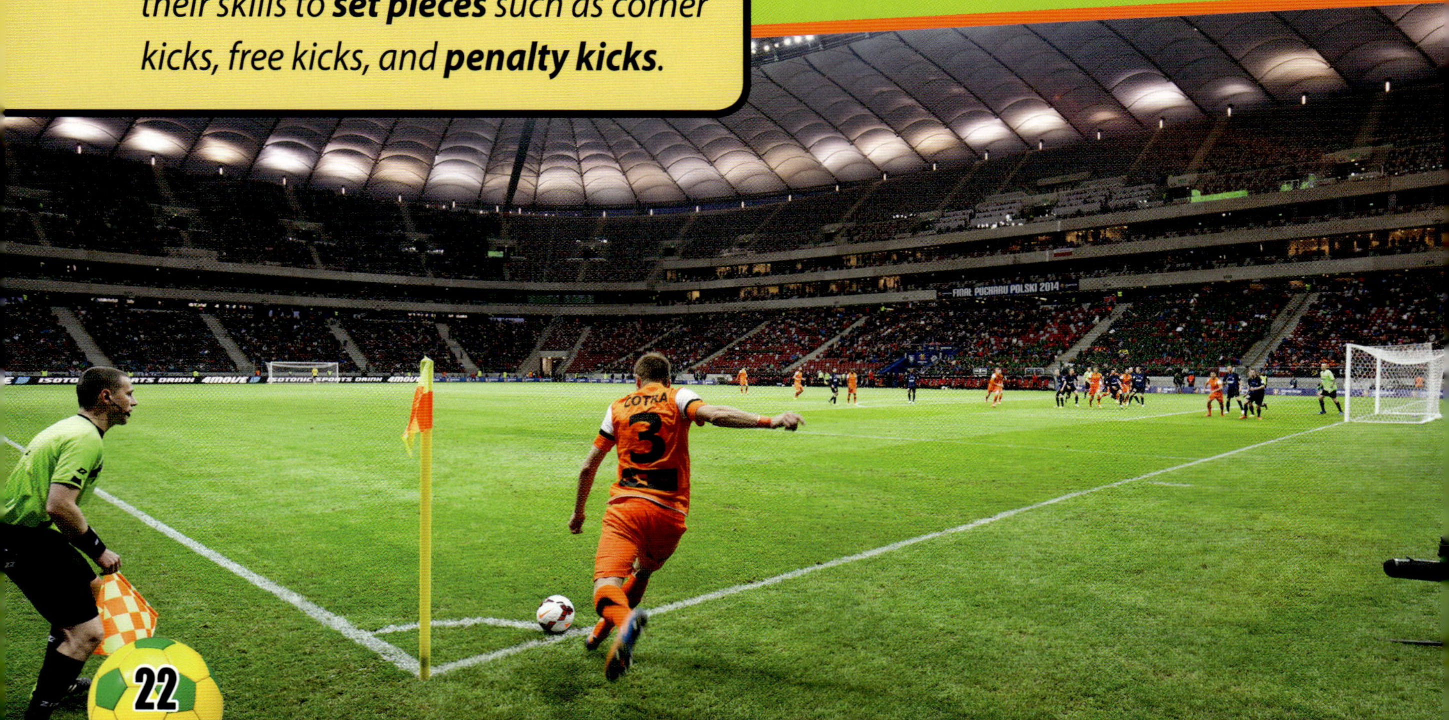

Although the term is not really meant as a compliment, fans of goal poachers argue that the number one aim of a forward is to score goals — and these players certainly know how to do that, often late in a game when the result is on the line. The poacher's motto seems to be "better late than never." While they are often the first to admit that they may not be the hardest workers on the field, they certainly contribute to a team's effort with their knack for scoring!

It's a difficult skill to master, but many top goal scorers are able to bend their free kicks to fool goalkeepers. By kicking the ball off-center, an experienced player can make it curve as it flies through the air. This is especially useful when opponents set up a "wall" of two or more players to try to block the free kick, because a bending free kick can actually curve right around the wall and into the net!

THE ROLE OF A HEAD COACH

Head coaches have a very important job. They decide what formation and tactics a team will use, which 11 players will start a game, and which players will come in as substitutes. Head coaches have several assistant coaches who help them do their job. In soccer, the head coach is sometimes also known as the manager.

Head coaches are responsible for just about every important decision during a game. In all levels of soccer, it's common to see head coaches shouting instructions to players during the entire game.

DID YOU KNOW?

When a player scores three goals in a game, it's called a hat trick. The term actually comes from the sport of cricket, where fans would throw their hats on the field to celebrate a good performance. Every soccer forward wants to score a hat trick. The amazing Lionel Messi once scored a hat trick in only 12 minutes in a Spanish league game. He could have had even more goals, but stepped aside so his teammate Luis Suarez could take a penalty kick in a great display of team spirit.

In addition to leading the team during games, head coaches and their assistants are also responsible for setting up and running training sessions. Head and assistant coaches help players build their individual skills and practice team tactics. To prepare for games, head coaches often study videos of opposing teams to understand their strengths and weaknesses.

In professional soccer, head coaches must stay in one spot along the sideline. This is called the technical area and is located close to a team's bench. The only exception to this rule occurs when a head coach comes onto the field to help a player who has gone down with an injury, after play has stopped.

THE BEST FORWARDS

Famous forwards of the past include Miroslav Klose, who broke the all-time leading goal-scoring record in the World Cup finals in 2014 when he led Germany to victory. Argentina's Diego Maradona is often considered one of the top three players of all time in any position. He had an amazing array of dribbling skills and led his country to a World Cup win in 1986.

American Abby Wambach (right) has scored more international goals than any other woman or man in history, with a total of 184 goals. She is also the all-time leading goal scorer for Team USA. Neymar (left), who was born in Brazil, stars for both FC Barcelona and the Brazilian national team. He is known for his ability to dribble, finish, and handle the ball with both feet.

DID YOU KNOW?

Edson Arantes do Nascimento is better known to fans around the world as Pelé — and many of those fans consider him to be the best soccer player of all time. Pelé scored an amazing total of 1,281 goals for his club team in Brazil, the New York Cosmos, and the Brazilian national team. He helped Brazil to win three World Cups in 1958, 1962, and 1970, making him the only player to win this many. In 1999 he was voted World Player of the Century, as well as Athlete of the Century by the International Olympic Committee.

Brazilian forward Marta Vieira da Silva is often considered one of the best soccer players of all time. She is currently the all-time scoring leader in Women's World Cup history! American star Alex Morgan is a mainstay and regular goal scorer on the U.S. Women's National team, who also plays professionally in France.

English star Jamie Vardy (left) helped long shot Leicester City win the 2015–16 English Premier League with his lightning speed and superb goal-scoring skills. France's Antoine Griezmann (right) was the top scorer and was voted top player of the tournament at the 2016 European Championship — despite being told by many teams he was too small to be successful as a youngster.

BE A GOOD SPORT

One of the reasons soccer is called "the beautiful game" is the devotion its players, fans, officials, and coaches have to the principle of sportsmanship. For example, it is not uncommon for professional players to help an opponent who has fallen down up off the pitch. Strong teams often refuse to run up a big score against weaker teams, and players kick the ball out of bounds when an opponent is injured so they can receive treatment.

Young players should remember that it never hurts to give a big thanks to the people who help and support them in developing their skills and building their love of the game.

RESPECTING THE REFEREES

Referees try to do the best job they can, but they can make mistakes. Players, parents, and coaches should always respect the refs — no matter the level of play. Yelling at the refs or arguing calls is not good sportsmanship, and this behavior rarely helps a team. Also, it's important to keep in mind that in youth soccer, many referees are also young people just learning how to referee.

RESPECT

Soccer players know that teams who receive respectful treatment from opponents will also give that respect back. Of course, it is important for soccer players to give 100 percent effort in games and training, but trying to win should never be more important than showing respect for teammates and opponents.

Everyone on the field, on the bench, and in the stands wants to have a fair game where everyone is treated well.

GLOSSARY

assist Pass that leads directly to another player scoring a goal.

crosses Aerial passes, usually delivered from the wing with the intention of being headed on goal.

dribble To run with the ball under control at the feet.

false nine A soccer position that is a combination of striker and attacking midfielder.

goal poachers The nickname given to players with an instinct for being in the right place to score goals.

penalty kicks Direct shots at goal with no other players permitted to be between the kicker and the goalkeeper, awarded for a foul inside the penalty area.

set piece A term used in soccer that refers to a situation when the ball is returned to open play, for example, following a stoppage in a game.

volleying To kick the ball before it hits the ground.

FOR MORE INFORMATION

FURTHER READING

Doeden, Matt. *The World's Greatest Soccer Players*. Sports Illustrated, 2010.

Fishman, Jon M. *Abby Wambach*. Lerner Publications, 2014.

Hoena, Blake. *National Geographic Kids Everything Soccer: Score Tons of Photos, Facts, and Fun*. National Geographic Children's Books, 2014.

WEBSITES

Due to the changing nature of Internet links, PowerKids Press has developed an online list of websites related to the subject of this book. This site is updated regularly. Please use this link to access the list:

www.powerkidslinks.com/ss/forward

INDEX

A

aerial ball 19

B

Benzema, Karim 20

C

coaches 24, 25

corner kicks 12, 18, 22

D

defenders 4, 7, 8, 10, 11, 13, 14, 15, 16, 17, 18

defense 7, 17, 22

dribble 6, 8, 10, 21, 26

Drogba, Didier 21

F

false nine 20, 21

formation(s) 4, 7, 9, 24

free kicks 12, 18, 21, 22, 23

G

Giovinco, Sebastian 9

goalkeepers 4, 11, 23

goal poachers 22, 23

Griezmann, Antoine 27

H

hat trick 25

heading 12, 18, 21

M

Messi, Lionel 15, 20, 25

midfielder 20, 21

N

Neymar 26

P

pass(es) 10, 11, 13, 14, 15, 16, 17, 20, 21

Pelé 27

penalty kicks 22

pitch 5, 6, 8, 9, 16, 17, 28

R

referees 29

respect 29

Ronaldo, Cristiano 15

S

scoring 4, 7, 9, 11, 12, 13, 14, 15, 17, 20, 22, 23, 26, 27

sidelines 5, 14, 25

strategy 7

strike partnership 9

strikers 8, 9, 11, 12, 13, 17, 18, 19, 20, 22

T

target player 16, 17

tracking back 7

V

Vardy, Jamie 27

Vieira da Silva, Marta 27

volleying 12

W

Wambach, Abby 26

wingers 7, 8, 10, 14, 15